EFT Tapping

How To Relieve Stress And Re-Energise Rapidly Using The Emotional Freedom Technique (Beginners Guide)

©2014 Colin G Smith

AwesomeMindSecrets.com

Disclaimer

This eBook is for educational purposes only, and is not intended to be a substitute for professional counselling, therapy or medical treatment. Nothing in this eBook is intended to diagnose or treat any pathology or diseased condition of the mind or body. The author will not be held responsible for any results of reading or applying the information.

Table of Contents

About Colin G Smith	4
Stress – The Modern Curse	5
The Energy Body	7
The Ultimate Self Help Tool	9
De-Stress Fast	11
Energy EFT Tapping Diagram	12
The Energy EFT Heart & Soul Tapping Sequence	13
Stress Reduction - Energy Tapping Sequence	16
Rapid Stress Relief Is Now In Your Hands	18
The Daily De-Stress Dojo	19
What To Do If You Get Stuck On The SUE Scale	20
How To Re-Energise Rapidly	22
Re-Energise Rapidly Tapping Sequence	23
The +10 Mind-Set	25
EFT Frequently Asked Questions	28
Q. Is EFT Safe?	28
Q. Is EFT simply a placebo or distraction from the problem?	28
Q. What about when EFT doesn't seem to work?	28
Q. Why do I have to focus on the negative?	28
Q. How hard should I tap?	28
Q. What are some of the signs of energy releasing?	29
Q. How will I know if it's working?	29
EFT Tapping Best Practice Checklist:	30

About Colin G Smith

For over ten years now I have been driven to find the very best methods for creating effective personal change. If you are anything like me, you're probably interested in simple and straight-forward explanations. Practical stuff that gets results! I am a NLP Master Practitioner, writer & author who has written several books including:

- *Boost Your Mind Power: 99+ Awesome Mind Power Techniques*
- *How To Meditate: Meditation Techniques For Beginners Guide Book*
- *Creative Problem Solving Techniques To Change Your Life*

Visit My Amazon Author Page:
www.amazon.com/author/colingsmith

Stress – The Modern Curse

These days everyone is suffering from stress. It has actually become normal to feel some kind of background stress most of the time. It's not healthy and it's far from the optimal state a human being can achieve. We all know the symptoms of stress: *aches and pains, tension headaches, stomach upset, fatigue, feeling overwhelmed, irritability, anxiousness, memory problems, lack of concentration* and so forth...

We know the use of drugs often cause further problems. The so called *side effect!* Relaxation techniques are a good idea such as daily meditation. However, have you got the time to really allow your mind to settle down into the zone? Have you ever tried to meditate but been too stressed out in the first place to settle your mind? What is needed is something that is both simple and effective that we put to use right away – **FAST!**

Well, I'm here to present you with the good news. In the last couple of decades, there has been a remarkable break-through discovery. A paradigm shifting new field of personal growth that transcends just *Mind & Body* change-work into the all encompassing Spirit(ual) or energetic level of change.

Old School Personal Change-Work

Many change-workers are still using traditional approaches to personal change such as exploring the root cause of problems in people's childhood. This can cause unnecessary pain and upset and more often than not doesn't heal the pain!

The New Paradigm

The modern, cutting edge personal change methods you are going to discover as you read on are based on a simple yet profound premise:

All the emotional disturbances you experience are due to blocks in the flow of energy in your Energy Body.

The Energy Body

Human beings have an energy body that energy flows through. Your thoughts and emotions are governed by this flow of energy. If there are blocks getting in the way of the free flow of energy, like boulders in a river, they will manifest in your mind and body as negative emotions and physical pain. The good news is you can clear up disturbances in the energy field quite rapidly and this in turn balances your emotions.

Mind	Body	Spirit (Energy Body)
Psychology	Physiology	Energy

Of course, ancient civilisations had knowledge about the body's energy system. The most well-known being Acupuncture which can be traced back several thousand years. Acupuncture works by placing needles strategically on the meridian lines (energy pathways) to unblock stagnant energy. This process can also be done using the fingers to touch the Acupoints. It was from experimenting with Acupressure that Psychologist, Dr. Roger Callahan, made a break through discovery.

He had been working with a client for 18 months trying to resolve her extreme phobia of water. It was so bad she even experienced terrors when bathing in a mere 2 inches of water! He had tried everything in the therapist bag, including non-standard psychology techniques such as Hypnosis. The breakthrough finally came when he asked the client to tap under her eye (which is an important Acupressure/Meridian Point) and her fear disappeared spontaneously and never returned.

Dr. Callahan then worked on this approach and developed Thought Field Therapy (TFT), which was based on the idea that thoughts are related to the energy field of the body and that by changing the energy field, by tapping on the Acupoints, you could release negative emotions quickly.

As he developed the TFT protocol and achieved more consistent results he started teaching the method to others. One of his students in the early 90's, Gary Craig, streamlined the process and made it more accessible for everyday people to use on themselves and others for freeing themselves of negative emotions. He named the method, **Emotional Freedom Techniques** or **EFT** for short. This has become quite well known, due to being shared freely on the internet and the fact that it is so effective. It is now used as a self help tool all over the world.

Because of the association and roots with psychology, psychologists and therapists, TFT, EFT and numerous other *Tapping Techniques* became known as the Energy Psychology field. However, Dr. Silvia Hartmann, Director of the Association for Meridian Therapies (The AMT), points out that modern energy work is no longer an adjunct of Psychology. It is a field in its own right. Not mind. Not Body. But Spirit.

> *"The third field addresses neither mental health, nor physical health, but instead the important topic of energy body health and well-being, which is foundational and without which a truly holistic treatment of many, if not all, human problems simply cannot exist."* - Dr. Silvia Hartmann

The Ultimate Self Help Tool

Energy EFT Tapping is the ultimate self help tool because it's so easy to do and highly effective.

Other benefits include:
- No religious connotations
- It's literally within your own hands!
- Know Thy Self – increase your emotional intelligence
- Discover your patterns

The Subjective Units of Discomfort/Distress/Disturbance (SUD) Scale is used to measure the level of a person's pain on a scale from -10 to 0. This was adopted in Energy Psychology circles to gauge where they were in the treatment process for neutralising a negative emotion to zero. In 2009, Dr. Hartmann updated this useful tool into something simple yet quite profound. I introduce you to, The Subjective Units of <u>Experience</u> or **SUE Scale**:

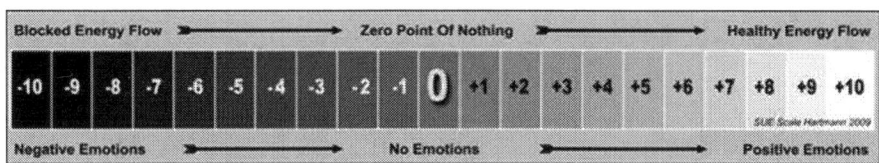

So as you can see a positive +1 to +10 has been added to the scale. Now at first glance you can be forgiven for thinking, *"well so what, what's the big deal?!"* Nevertheless as you'll begin to see, the SUE Scale gives us an amazing, empowering way of engaging in personal transformation.

Getting to Zero(0) is simply not good enough!

That's the starting point. First, we release the stress. AND THEN we get into the good stuff! The positive, **energising emotions** such as *enthusiasm, inspiration, humour, love and playfulness!*

Our expectations about feeling good have been way too low for way too long. With Energy Tapping, we can quickly release the negative energy perturbations and blast into the *natural highs*. And we're talking minutes, not hours or weeks!

De-Stress Fast

"Sounds Good, I'm Ready To Give It A Shot."

Because we've been influenced by certain ideas and concepts about personal change for so long in our culture, I'm going to remind you of the most important premise in the new paradigm of personal change. In fact, I strongly suggest you write it out in big letters and put it somewhere prominent because our conditioning can be so ingrained we need to remind ourselves regularly of this new paradigm:

> *All the emotional disturbances you experience are due to blocks in the flow of energy in your Energy Body.*

When we adopt this attitude, personal change-work becomes easier and more fun. Now you're actually going to learn an Energy Tapping procedure for reducing stress quickly and easily. There are different *Tapping Algorithms* out there, but I like the AMT's, "*Energy EFT Heart & Soul*" protocol, simply because it is so simple and effective.

Have a look at the diagram below...

Energy EFT Tapping Diagram

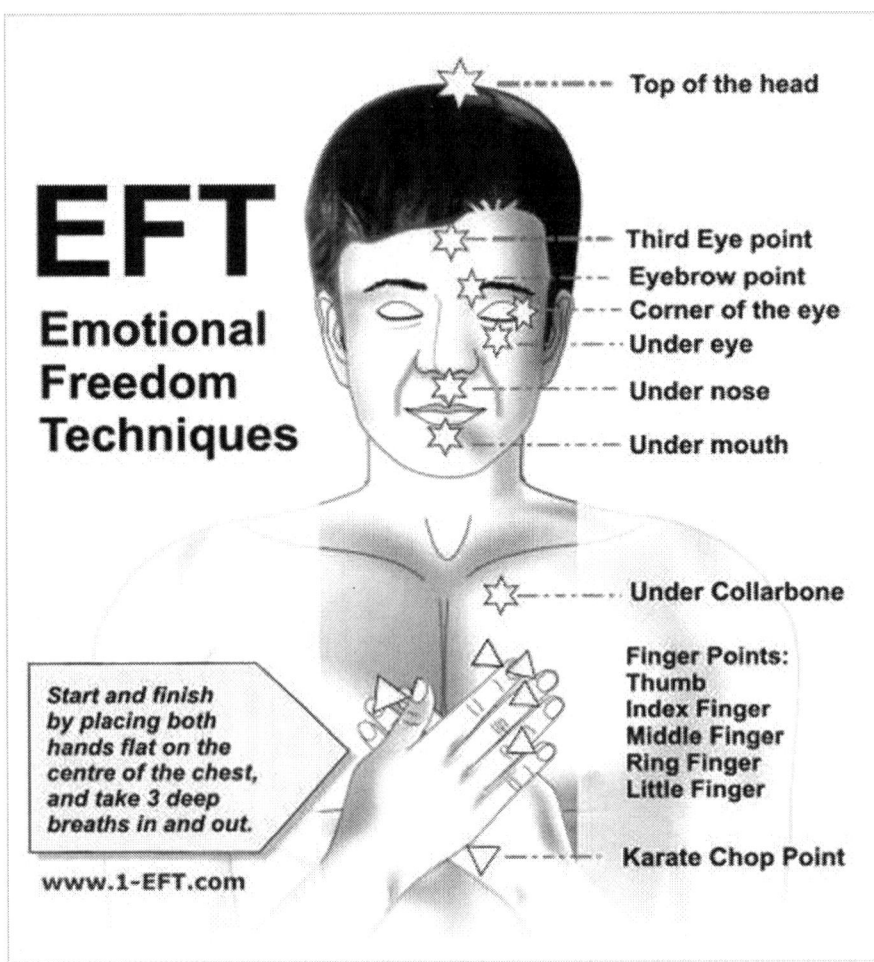

The Energy EFT Heart & Soul Tapping Sequence

EFT uses major energy centres and special energy points or meridian points to stimulate and improve the flow of energy through the energy body.

0 = The Heart Centre. This is where we start and finish our round of EFT by placing both hands flat on the centre of the chest in the Heart Healing Position and take three deep breaths in and out.

1. Top Of The Head - The highest point on the top of your head.

2. Third Eye Point - In the centre of your forehead.

3. Start Of The Eyebrow - Where the bone behind your eyebrow turns into the bridge of your nose.

4. Corner Of The Eye - On the bone in the corner of your eye.

5. Under The Eye - On the bone just below your eye, in line with your pupil if you look straight ahead.

6. Under The Nose - Between you nose and your upper lip

7. Under The Mouth - In the indentation between your chin and your lower lip

8. Under The Collarbone - In the angle formed by your collarbone and the breastbone

9. Thumb - all finger points are on the side of the finger, in line with the nail bed.

10. Index Finger

11. Middle Finger

12. Ring Finger

13. Little Finger

14. Karate Chop Point - on the side of your hand, roughly in line with your life line.

0 = And to finish the round of EFT, back to the Heart Healing Position where we take three deep breaths in and out.

*This sequence is an extract from: energyeft.com/Energy_EFT.htm

Take a moment now to go through the sequence, starting with the Heart Healing position where you take three deep breaths in and out.

Then find and touch each point in turn with your index finger.

Touch each point lightly, breathe deeply and simply pay attention to how the sensation feels, and how each point creates all kinds of different sensations you can feel in your body. If this protocol is new to you, practice it for a few days so you are familiar with how it works.

> *"Energy Flows, Where Attention Goes"*

When you've been through the sequence a few times you'll soon get the hang of it and be able to do it easily. You may have noticed yourself becoming more relaxed just by practising going through the sequence. The next ingredient we will add into the mix will help to reduce stress much more rapidly.

The Set-Up Phrase

Because the aim of Energy Tapping is to increase the flow of energy in the energy body and release blockages, we focus the energy intervention with our intention and attention. It's really quite straight forward...

Starting at Step 0, the *Hands On Heart* position we simply state out loud or just in our head, *"I want to release this stress,"* three times, complete with the deep breaths in and out.

That's it! You've Set-Up the intention and attention.

The Reminder Phrase

You would now move on to Step 1, Top Of The Head:

Breathing in a deep breath, touch or tap the point while repeating the reminder phrase, ***"Stress."***

You then repeat this on the rest of the points in the sequence.

Breathing Magic

It's important to breathe deeply throughout the process because your breathing is closely related to the Energy Body. Breathing deeply helps get the life force energy moving in your system.

To Touch Or To Tap?

You now go through all the points in the sequence back to the hands on *Heart Healing Position*.

You can either just touch the points, as you breath in deeply, or you can tap them gently with your finger. There is something satisfying about tapping; it gives you a rhythm to move along too. You can do it quite fast, like the speed of the rhythm of *Jingle Bells*.

Keep in Mind: It is your Energy Hand tapping your Energy Body

When you've got used to the flow of the sequence you will be able to tap through a whole round in less than 3 minutes. I have repeated the sequence again for you below with the Set-Up of, "*Stress Reduction*" to help further clarify the process...

Stress Reduction - Energy Tapping Sequence

The Set-Up Phrase, *"I want to release this stress"*

The Reminder Phrase, *"Stress"*

0 = The Heart Centre. Take three deep breaths in and out while repeating, *"I want to release this stress."*

Now tap on the following points while repeating the reminder phrase, *"Stress."* Remember to breath in and out, deeply, at each point:

1. Top Of The Head - "Stress"

2. Third Eye Point - "Stress"

3. Start Of The Eyebrow - "Stress"

4. Corner Of The Eye - "Stress"

5. Under The Eye - "Stress"

6. Under The Nose - "Stress"

7. Under The Mouth - "Stress"

8. Under The Collarbone - "Stress"

9. Thumb - "Stress"

10. Index Finger - "Stress"

11. Middle Finger - "Stress"

12. Ring Finger - "Stress"

13. Little Finger - "Stress"

14. Karate Chop Point - "Stress"

0 = And to finish the round of EFT, back to the Heart Healing Position where we take three deep breaths in and out while repeating, *"I want to release this stress."*

Subsequent Rounds: Take a new SUE Scale reading and then update your Set-Up Phrase to something such as, *"I release this remaining stress."*

Rapid Stress Relief Is Now In Your Hands

You have now learned the main process. Pretty simple right? So let's get right into how you can use this process for rapid stress relief in the real world.

Remember this? (*Well, this is actually the fun, smiley version!*)

OK, so right now, go ahead and notice how stressed you are at this very moment. You may be surprised. Everyone is suffering from stress these days. Of course, it fluctuates throughout the day. Simply notice where you are currently on the scale.

Now go through the tapping sequence. Then notice how you feel.

It's probably not at the Zero point just yet, so tap another round with a new Set-Up Phrase such as, *"I release this remaining stress."*

Keep going. Remember a full round only takes a couple of minutes!

Keep tapping until you get to Zero on the SUE scale.

Well done, you've just learned how to release stress – very quickly too!

The Daily De-Stress Dojo

One of the best things you can do for your health and well-being is to practice using this tool every day to reduce your general stress levels. By being consistent and persistent, you will help to reduce your background stress levels and raise your *baseline energy or vibration state*.

I suggest you get one of those index cards and write the days of the week along the top. Then have 3 rows for three sessions during each day. You can tick the box when you've done a 10, 15 or 20 minute de-stress / re-energising session.

Energy Tapping Top Tip!

Have you got a Smart Phone?

Get one of the Free Apps for a Stopwatch, Egg Timer or Meditation Timer. (*You can of course get one for your computer instead.*)

Now set the count down for 10, 15 or 20 Minutes depending on your schedule.

Start the Timer when you start your Energy Tapping session.

What To Do If You Get Stuck On The SUE Scale

So what do you do when you can't move up the SUE Scale. You've become stuck in the same position even though you persist with rounds of tapping. It happens sometimes. It's known as a *Psychological Reversal*. That's when there is a subconscious process that sabotages all progress.

I'm going to give you several methods to overcome the *stuck state*. The thing to keep in mind is that you always want to end a tapping session heading towards +10 !

> *All the emotional disturbances you experience are due to blocks in the flow of energy in your Energy Body.*

Hands On Heart Position: Always come back to this position if you ever feel stuck. Re-state your intention or set-up phrase and just breathe deeply for a few moments.

Deep Breathing While Tapping: Remember that your breathing is closely related to the flow of energy in your energy body.

Eyes Open / Closed: If you usually do the tapping with your eyes closed try doing it with them open and vice-versa.

Remember You're Tapping The <u>Energy Body</u>

Say The Phrases Out Loud

Swap Hands / Tap The Other Side Of Your Body / Try Both Sides Simultaneously

Drink Some Water

Chose Another Word That's More Emotive For You: For example try, *"I'm going out of my frickin mind!"* instead of using the word

"Stress."

Move Around. Shake About.

Body Sensations: Notice where the feelings are in your body. Are the feelings in your stomach, chest or head? Now try tapping on *"this feeling"* or *"this body sensation."*

Metaphor: Using Metaphorical Imagery can be very powerful and fun! Ask yourself questions such as, *"What is this feeling like?" "If this feeling was a place in time and space what would it be?"*

Notice how the metaphors evolve with tapping and incorporate each change into your Set-Up Phrase. You can just use colours as symbols. What colour do you feel? e.g.) *"I feel grey."*

The Insights Points: Try just putting your fingers on the Insight Points: The start of the eyebrow. Breathe deeply as you touch this point. Notice any shifts in your awareness of energy, feelings, thoughts and internal imagery. Swap to the other eye's insight point and repeat the process a few times. (*I learned this from Zivorad Mihajlovic Slavinski's excellent Primordial Energy Activation and Transcendence or PEAT System. I highly recommend his materials.*)

Timer Tricks: When we're really stressed out, we can't be bothered to do the exercises. So set your Timer to just 5 minutes and get tapping! It's likely that something will shift and you will then have the impetuous to continue towards the +10's.

How To Re-Energise Rapidly

OK, so you've released the stress and reached the *Zero Point of Nothing*, which is great, but now the **real magic** happens when you tap yourself into the **Positive Emotional Energy Flows!**

This is where the simplicity and profundity of the SUE Scale takes you off into a new way of living. It will help you develop a new approach to life. A very healthy Mind-Set. One of striving for more and more positive energy states, more consistently and more powerfully! Of course, that can only be a good thing for you, your loved ones and everyone that comes into your presence can it not?

So you've tapped into the *Zero-Point*. You now <u>choose</u> a new Set-Up Phrase. What do you want to experience more? What positive states do you want to feel?

    e.g.) *"I want to feel amazing!"*

    e.g.) *"I want to feel energised!"*

    e.g.) *"I want to feel loving"*

    e.g.) *"I have a great sense of humour!"*

    e.g.) *"I have a Heart of Gold!"*

You now go through the Tapping Sequence with the new positive set up phrase. Keep tapping and repeating the full sequence and notice how your feelings are expanding on the SUE scale as you become more energised!

Aim to getting so amazingly high you are at a +10

Re-Energise Rapidly Tapping Sequence

The Set-Up Phrase, *"I want to feel really energised!"*

The Reminder Phrase, *"Really energised!"*

0 = The Heart Centre. Take three deep breaths in and out while repeating, *"I want to feel really energised!"*

Now tap on the following points while repeating the reminder phrase, *"Really energised!"* Remember to breathe in and out, deeply, at each point:

1. Top Of The Head - "Really energised!"

2. Third Eye Point - "Really energised!"

3. Start Of The Eyebrow - "Really energised!"

4. Corner Of The Eye - "Really energised!"

5. Under The Eye - "Really energised!"

6. Under The Nose - "Really energised!"

7. Under The Mouth - "Really energised!"

8. Under The Collarbone - "Really energised!"

9. Thumb - "Really energised!"

10. Index Finger - "Really energised!"

11. Middle Finger - "Really energised!"

12. Ring Finger - "Really energised!"

13. Little Finger - "Really energised!"

14. Karate Chop Point - "Really energised!"

0 = And to finish the round of EFT, back to the Heart Healing Position where we take three deep breaths in and out while repeating, *"I want to feel really energised!"*

Subsequent Rounds: Take a new SUE Scale reading and then update your Set-Up Phrase to something such as, *"I want to feel **even more** energised!"*

The +10 Mind-Set

As you energise yourself by tapping in positive states, you may find at some point you can't seem to move up any higher on the SUE scale. Remember we're heading towards a +10 every time we do a round of tapping. This is where it gets really interesting. By practising this process, one of the side benefits is that you will gain new insights into what _really_ makes you feel good.

When you want to feel even better and continue moving up the scale, ask yourself one of the following kinds of question:

- *"What else do I need, right now, to feel really happy and fully energised?"*
- *"What do I need to experience to get to +10?"*
- *"Just imagine if you could feel even better, what would get you there?"*
- *"What else do I need to experience right now to be really happy?"*

One of the things I've noticed when practising this process is that one of the common *psychological reversals* can appear: Deservedness.

Fortunately, there is a simple solution. When starting your positive energising tapping simply do a few rounds with this set-up, *"I deserve to be _really_ happy and healthy."* (Of course, you can word it with something more meaningful for you if you so wish.)

Make It A Habit!

Once you get into *Energy Tapping* you will find it invaluable in your everyday life. It's a great way to start the day. When you've de-stressed, you can think about what tasks you've got coming up. As you do so, you should choose what resourceful states of mind you would like to be in. You then tap them in...

Enthusiasm, Creativity, Resourcefulness, Playfulness, Focus, Motivation, Passion, Joyfulness...

To help you get into it, you might find it useful to write out a simple weekly schedule on an index card. Simply write the days of the week along the top and then have say, three rows for morning, midday and afternoon. Tick the box when you've done a de-stress / re-energising session.

Remember it only takes about 15 minutes and it is **well worth it!**

Taking It Further

You can do many wonderful things with Energy EFT. What you've learned in this book is just the tip of the iceberg. Being able to de-stress at will is very useful and essential today. However, you can explore the vastness of human consciousness when you get into tapping the positive side of the SUE Scale. What states of mind could you achieve if you allowed yourself?!

What would happen if you tapped, *"I am a creative genius,"* to the level of +10 ?

Moreover, what about:

- *"I have a really bright, compelling future!"*
- *"Anything is possible."*
- *"I feel incredibly empowered."*

Maybe you're interested in exploring the spiritual dimensions of human experience?

- *"I feel an incredible connection with Infinite Intelligence."*
- *"I feel completely at one with the Universe."*
- *"I am pure love."*

If you want to explore Energy EFT in more depth and discover the wide range of practical applications for this wonderment, I highly recommend you get a copy of <u>Dr. Silvia Hartmann's book, "Energy EFT."</u> It's a <u>must read</u> if you're truly interested in learning more about *Energy Tapping*.

Other Books about EFT worth reading:

The Tapping Solution: A Revolutionary System for Stress-Free Living by Nick Ortner

Matrix Reimprinting Using EFT: Rewrite Your Past, Transform Your Future by Karl Dawson and Sasha Allenby

EFT Frequently Asked Questions

Q. Is EFT Safe?

Yes, EFT is completely safe and there are no known negative side effects.

Q. Is EFT simply a placebo or distraction from the problem?

No. The placebo effect requires some belief in the process and this isn't usually the case for people new to EFT. Although EFT could appear to be distracting, it will not work properly if the person is actually distracted. That is why we continually repeat a reminder phrase to keep us tuned in to the core of the problem.

Q. What about when EFT doesn't seem to work?

Go to the chapter titled, *"What To Do If You Get Stuck On The SUE Scale."*

Q. Why do I have to focus on the negative?

You don't have to. As described in the book it's good to reduce your stress level down to the zero point on the SUE scale before tapping in positive resourceful states. Nevertheless you could simply start tapping on the Positives if you wanted. e.g.) *"I am feeling really energised."*

Q. How hard should I tap?

Keep in mind you are really tapping your subtle energy body. So you don't need to tap hard. Tap in a way that is similar to you gently drumming your finger on a table. The speed of the tapping is like the rhythm of Jingle Bells.

Q. What are some of the signs of energy releasing?

You may notice the following:

- Yawning
- Sighs
- Tears
- Giggling
- You might feel more energised or more tired
- The feeling may shift in the way it feels or the feeling could move to another part of your body

Q. How will I know if it's working?

The SUE scale will help you notice if it is working or not. Let's say you started out feeling quite stressed at a -4 on the scale. You then started rounds of tapping and checked the SUE scale again and noticed you were now at a -2. Great! Continue tapping, changing your Set Up Phrase if necessary, until you are feeling really good heading towards the +10 on the SUE scale.

EFT Tapping Best Practice Checklist:

- SUE Scale: Check where you are on the scale
- Set Up Phrase: Come up with your Set Up Phrase. e.g.) "*I want to release this stress*"
- Speed of Tapping: Like the speed of the rhythm of Jingle Bells.
- Breathing: Remember to breathe deeply
- Keep Tapping until you get to the Zero Point of Nothing (*It only takes a few minutes.*)
- Now begin tapping a Positive high up the SUE scale (*Aim to get to +10.*)
- Drink some water: It helps the shifts you've created in the bodies energy fields.

Printed in Great Britain
by Amazon